New Management

B. Vincent

Published by RWG Publishing, 2021.

While every precaution has been taken in the preparation of this book, the publisher assumes no responsibility for errors or omissions, or for damages resulting from the use of the information contained herein.

NEW MANAGEMENT

First edition. August 9, 2021.

Copyright © 2021 B. Vincent.

Written by B. Vincent.

Also by B. Vincent

Affiliate Marketing
Affiliate Marketing
Affiliate Marketing

Standalone
Business Employee Discipline
Affiliate Recruiting
Business Layoffs & Firings
Business and Entrepreneur Guide
Business Remote Workforce
Career Transition
Project Management
Precision Targeting
Professional Development
Strategic Planning
Content Marketing
Imminent List Building
Getting Past GateKeepers
Banner Ads

Bookkeeping
Bridge Pages
Business Acquisition
Business Bogging
Marketing Automation
Better Meetings
Conversion Optimization
Creative Solutions
Employee Recruitment
Startup Capital
Employee Mentoring
Followership
Servant Leadership
Human Resources
Team Building
Freelancing
Funnel Building
Geo Targeting
Goal Setting
Immanent List Building
Lead Generation
Leadership Course
Leadership Transition
LinkedIn Ads
LinkedIn Marketing
New Management

New Management

Henry Mintzberg once said the executives is most importantly, a training where craftsmanship science and specialty meet. Turning into a decent supervisor is maybe perhaps the most troublesome ranges of abilities to grow reliably and apply on an everyday premise. That is on the grounds that it's a training comprised of many disciplines. Without a doubt, to be a decent administrator, you should be a decent pioneer. That is, you need to move, inspire, and impact. However, you additionally need to have a superb handle of different things like arranging, planning, restraining, appointing, and endless more. The achievement or disappointment of your association relies upon your capacity to ably adjust everything. Thus, there's no space for lack of energy, and no place for disappointment. In this course, we will assist you with that and leviathan of every one of my difficulties, being a decent administrator.

As indicated by an investigation from Gallup, half of workers quit their positions in light of their chief. Another online investigation by the Harris Poll showed that 24% of representatives would consider stopping if their chiefs don't give sufficient input, while 68% of the respondents from an overview by grasp announced that they feel satisfied when they get exact and steady criticism. Our course will comprise of a progression of basic conversation focuses. These are intended to cover this expansive subject as completely as conceivable to empower development in these crucial regions, and to work with a genuine and productive conversation inside your association about how you can each enhance this fundamental trademark both at work, and in your own lives overall. A portion of these will be really extended, and some will be generally direct and brief. Toward the finish of this guide, comes the main last advance.

Conversation time don't skirt this. This is the main piece of this preparation. At the point when you finish this course, you need to go through somewhere around an hour or thereabouts going over the inquiries we supply toward the end collectively. Whoever's the big enchilada in the gathering should assign a facilitator whose obligation it is that each question is covered, and that everybody time allowing, can express their opinion, ensure all commitments are esteemed, all ideas considered, and all feelings regarded.

In this way, we should move into the primary conversation point. Become more acquainted with your workers on an expert and individual level. Set aside the effort to study your workers, including their vocation objectives and individual interests. Become more acquainted with their connections and interests outside of work that make them remarkably what their identity is. Knowing them personally and not similarly as a representative will assist you with understanding them more and influence that data to assist them with succeeding work. Representative a portion of your work. Many individuals who get elevated to administrative positions frequently attempted to do everything without anyone else and take on more work. Nonetheless, powerful directors comprehend the benefit of appointing, doled out undertakings and obligations to your colleague with the right arrangement of abilities and viewpoint to take care of business right and on schedule. In the event that nobody realizes how to do the work, set aside some effort to educate them. Your time is better spent on more significant errands. Rather than routine errands that any other person in your group can undoubtedly learn and achieve. Show others how it's done. Be a pioneer and not simply a director. Turn your group's inspiration towards an unmistakable bearing and objective. Show them how they can be effective inside the association by allowing them to gain from your model. In the event that you have elevated expectations for your group, work morally and inside tech Don't play top picks or single out explicit representatives for particular sorts of errands or activities. Develop trust by showing that you additionally have the characteristics that you need your colleagues to have. Be a viable communicator. Speaking with your colleagues is perhaps the main abilities that you need to know as a director. It's difficult to lead and deal with your group successfully. In the event that you can't propel individuals, cause them to comprehend your vision, or give criticism appropriately. Here are a few hints to assist with further developing your correspondence style. Set up your focuses ahead of time, and work on saying them so anyone can hear. set clear assumptions and explicit due dates. Try not to make your workers set out to find the real story. Continuously keep your group refreshed with what's going on in the organization and any likely arrangements. Your straightforwardness will cultivate a comprehensive culture where they will not be hesitant to voice their interests, conclusions, and thoughts. Be available to conversations and energize unique reasoning and inventiveness.

Figure out how to tune in. Driving requires learning and learning includes tuning in. As an administrator you ought to never cause your representatives to feel that they can't talk their assessment or add to good change in the association. At the point when you tune in and let your colleagues articulate their thoughts, you recognize them and furthermore acquire further experiences. following are a few hints to assist you with tuning in and keep a receptive outlook. Viable listening abilities include five parts getting, getting, recalling, surveying, and reacting. Go through these parts individually at whatever point you are conversing with a worker. Be mindful, keep in touch, take notes when fundamental, and sit tight for them to wrap up. Before you begin talking. Relinquish your assumptions. What's more, don't make hasty judgments previously or during the discussion. Tune in determined to know however much you can about the circumstance. Plan for conversations and gatherings. In any case, never accept that you know what your representatives are thinking what the issue is, for sure the arrangement is. Recognize achievement. commend the accomplishment of your group perceive their accomplishments and let them know how they had the option to contribute decidedly to the association. Try not to get hung up on what's missing for sure they couldn't achieve and zero in rather on their diligent effort. As indicated by an investigation by the Harvard Business Review, high performing groups have a proportion of six positive remarks to each one bad analysis. Recognition is an amazing help. What's more, some of the time it can even be superior to cash. It makes workers realize that they progressed nicely and urge them to improve later on. rouse your group. The capacity to rouse others is perhaps the best characteristics for any administrator. Your colleagues ought to have a positive confidence in the thoughts and assignments that you were requesting that they do. They shouldn't imagine that these assignments will achieve below average outcomes. At the point when the air at work is positive, assurance and efficiency will likewise increment. Here are a few things that you can attempt to spur your group. Ensure that every colleague their job. Furnish your representatives with a reasonable arrangement of objectives and a comprehension of how to achieve them. Guarantee that they have the offices and apparatuses to guarantee that objectives are reached on schedule. screen their achievements en route. Sort out what spurs your colleagues. Do they incline toward consistent input, calm appreciation, additional difficult ventures, or outside acknowledgment? Ensure that they are paid what they're worth. You would prefer not to lose high performing colleagues since they're being come up short on. energize coordinated effort and collaboration so everyone feels like they depend in the group for help and help. This will ingrain in them a more prominent connection to the accomplishments of your group and the organization. practice limitation. It's not difficult to let the pressure at work outwit you. You may be enticed to let out your dissatisfactions on your representatives. Yet, recollect that you'll need to manage unmotivated representatives will be prepared to leave at the principal opportunity to get control over your temper. Stay quiet and thoroughly consider things. In case you were a representative, you additionally wouldn't be glad to work at where the administrator gets handily incited, and consistently has something unsavory to say. practice a little tolerance, and rather than spinning out of control immediately, listen quietly to the current issue and offer sound exhortation and backing.

Practice self-reflection. successful pioneers are mindful, it's difficult to oversee others when you can't oversee yourself. Put away some an ideal opportunity to consider your activities, responses, and future drives. This can come in many structures, incorporating ordinary directing meetings with your supervisor exploring in different initiative methods, or getting some information about how you can improve. Recall that you shouldn't be so centered around others that you disregard yourself. Quiet down, think about your qualities and shortcomings, and recognize a strategy to assist with further developing those regions you need to chip away at. put out clear objectives and expectations. Objective setting is one of the signs of powerful supervisors, you need to have a reasonable vision and system for your group. Clear and obvious objectives won't simply fill in as a guide for the work that should be done yet will induce a common feeling of direction in your staff. While making the objectives for your group. Remember the accompanying. Every objective ought to be connected to a bunch of expectations which are basically little, noteworthy assignments. expectations will assist your workers with bettering their individual commitment tie into the greater objectives of the association. Try to repeat these objectives and expectations at each achievement, screen their advancement to guarantee that things keep focused. Timetable a one-on-one gathering where you can offer them guidance on dealing with specific undertakings are circumstances. Stay away from uncertain phrasing and put out SMART objectives that get continually refreshed and assessed.

Consider your colleagues responsible. Responsibility doesn't simply include considering your subordinates answerable for their work and their activities. All things considered;

responsibility should stream every which way inside the association. Every individual from the association should consider each other responsible, remembering those for the upper positions. Assuming you need to consider your group responsible to their errands, ensure that you impart this as unmistakably as could be expected. list down the normal results, consummation dates, and whatever other detail that they should focus on measure results with right and complete information that is likewise accessible to the remainder of the group. be comprehensive. support the entirety of your colleagues to add to arriving at the group's objective. Don't simply depend on specific individuals to achieve the most pivotal errands. You would prefer not to bar your representatives from undertakings that they may likewise be qualified and talented enough to do before you apportion work. Ensure that you consider their assessments and thoughts. Don't simply pass out directions to your colleagues without acquiring their criticism or allowing them to get what the assignment involves. Indeed, even the most current colleague demonstrates to have an extremely valuable or savvy idea. Establish a cooperative climate.

A community climate is one where every one of the individuals from the group feels regarded and esteemed. You can accomplish a community-oriented work environment by allowing your subordinates to see your own enthusiasm and energy for your work. Simultaneously, don't attempt to hold practically everything. All things being equal, assign and empower correspondence through input and normal one on one gatherings. Ensure that you underscore the significance of an inviting and strong air at work. characterize achievement. Achievement can be characterized subjectively or quantitatively.

The previous is estimated by perceptions and spotlight more on delicate abilities like adaptability, correspondence, or cooperation. The last is estimated by measurements or insights for each venture that you take in as a group It's significant for you to survey your group's exhibition through the two sorts of estimations. Quantitative execution assessments are unprejudiced and objective and are explicitly intended for the representative's job. A portion of your colleagues might be more open to seeing the results of their work clearly. Then again, subjective execution assessments are ideal for jobs where achievement can be somewhat more theoretical.

Oversee conduct. Overseeing conduct may seem like something out of a kindergarten instructors' rundown of undertakings, however compelling administrators comprehend its significance in the association. As a supervisor, you need to be sure that your representatives act in a manner that lines up with the association's qualities, and friend's culture. You must ensure that your colleagues comprehend the significance of your organization esteems, and that compromising these qualities is never to their greatest advantage. Overseeing worker conduct will likewise assist you with making a useful and successful working environment that will at last drive your association in front of the opposition. Take an initiative course, pioneers aren't conceived they're made. effectively dealing with further developing your administration abilities will make you a more powerful director. In any case, it's difficult to develop your own. What's more, in some cases it's smarter to request master counsel and help. One approach to do this is to take on an authority preparing program.

There are different online video-based courses that will make this cycle simpler for you. Some of them are free, albeit the more famous ones are offered at reasonable rates. They remember courses for basic reasoning, dynamic, how to make change, and how to differ appropriately. be straightforward. As per the American Psychological Association, around 25% of workers don't confide in their managers. As a supervisor. You don't need workers who don't confide in you or the organization, since they are probably not going to adjust their very own objectives to that of the organization. Here are some extraordinary tips that you can use to advance straightforwardness at work. In case there are any road obstructions that they might experience throughout their work, let them think about it, present thoughts also on how they can deal with these detours. In the event that you've gotten indispensable, however not secret data from senior administration, ensure that your group thinks about it too. Clarify the reasoning behind your choices so they are not left pondering about your reasons and inspirations. Try not to be hesitant to be the unfortunate messenger. It's certainly not a wonderful encounter. However, your colleagues should think about both the great and the awful to assist them with changing and improve constantly. Make an input framework. carry out a framework where your colleagues can give you input on the work that they are doing. opportune and reliable criticism from your subordinates will assist you with distinguishing shortcomings or unfriendly conduct just as build up sure ones. Your representatives should realize that they are allowed to communicate their thoughts when they feel that something's incorrectly. You can give holding one a shot one gatherings or an unknown idea box where your colleagues can tell you how you were doing as their chief.

Adjusted recognition and analysis. Your colleagues need a good arrangement of commendation and analysis to prevail in their jobs. On the off chance that you just give acclaim, you're not actually assisting your workers with developing. In any case, in the event that you just offer analysis, your workers will get dispirited and be continually anxious. Attempt the accompanying tips in case you are fostering a framework for giving helpful remarks give more applause than analysis. Exploration from the Harvard Business Review showed that top performing groups ordinarily have a consistent and ceaseless progression of positive remarks. never lie to your colleagues about how they're doing. Sort out when where and how to give acclaim appropriately. great outcomes and conduct ought to be recognized and remunerated reliably and instantly. Recall that public and private commendation just as exceptional acknowledgments are incredible administration devices for building trust and spirit. Analysis should likewise be ideal. Notwithstanding, you shouldn't simply recognize their mix-ups. give them criticism that will assist them with conquering their shortcomings. By permitting to define objectives for development. You're showing your conviction and their capacities and abilities. Continuously finish on a positive note. Be explicit while remarking on their work. Rather than simply revealing to them that they're working effectively, notice a particular undertaking and let them know why their activities or endeavors were praiseworthy.

Give mentorship or profession advancement freedoms to raise spirit and spur your group to accomplish more prominent statures. Your representatives need to feel that they are filling in their jobs and learning new things. They ought to have the option to see short-and long-haul profession openings that will empower them to arrive at their maximum capacity. Else, they'll doubtlessly be searching for better freedoms somewhere else. Set aside the effort to set out improvement open doors that would help each staff part progress on their individual vocation ways. In the event that you don't have the spending plan for huge scope meetings or trainings, consider getting more senior workers in the association to coach your colleagues and help with their profession objectives. Utilize stretch tasks to challenge your group. A stretch task is one that includes abilities or information that is past the current collection of a worker. To help your colleagues master new abilities and help them handle work outside of their usual range of familiarity. Take a stab at allotting stretch tasks from time to time. Here are a portion of the top motivations to utilize stretch tasks. Decide if a worker can possibly take on positions of authority and more obligations. Set up your group to move forward when you are nowhere to be found. test groundbreaking thoughts, ideas, and approaches. Guarantee that you'll have labor if the association chooses to grow in the new projects and undertakings. open your group to different offices and spaces of the association.

Don't micromanage micromanaging happens when directors attempt to actually control each part of a staff individuals work. This frequently implies that the administrator will forget about the master plan and spotlight a lot on the subtleties. micromanagement is outlandish and disheartening on the grounds that your workers will not have any opportunity to have an independent perspective and settle on autonomous choices.

Here are a portion of the risks of micromanagement. At the point when you definitely limit your administration style, you likewise limit your method for correspondence and at last, your administration capacity. Your workers lose their confidence in you. They'll at this point don't consider you to be a director. Be that as it may, as somebody who ingrains dread and nervousness. Your workers will lose the certainty to do jobs all alone and rather become intensely reliant upon you and your steady impedance. you'll rapidly wear out micromanagement is debilitating, and the work will ultimately get to you. It might even reason you to detest your work, and surprisingly the association that utilizes you make a worker acknowledgment framework. being held in high regard by your companions persuades a representative to work more enthusiastically and causes them to feel that they are an extraordinary fit for the association. A worker acknowledgment framework recognizes the commitments of a staff part to the objectives of the organization and lauds their excellent exhibition. In case you are intending to foster an acknowledgment framework for your own group, here are some cool thoughts that you can test. Money related rewards will consistently cause a representative to feel esteemed on the grounds that it shows that their diligent effort is paying off.

Part with custom gifts or organization marked things like packs, tumblers, or shirts to workers who are performing admirably. plan a free lunch for your group to treat them for working really hard for the week. Commend work commemorations, birthday celebrations, and other critical life occasions with your colleagues. Ensure that everybody's qualified for the acknowledgment. try not to prohibit anybody or any gathering, particularly on the off chance that you deal with a group with fluctuating liabilities. You might need to consider making numerous acknowledgment programs for various kinds of jobs or positions. Make Work more fun. Probably the best organizations on the planet have made a working environment where representatives can remain cheerful and spurred. Ensure that you track down the right equilibrium so that while they can have a spot to clear their psyches and feel invigorated, they're as yet ready to remain connected with and useful.

Following are some good thoughts to make your office more fun. Have a little sporting facility, consider adding a sofa a few beanbags, an excursion seat, or a pool table. This will fill in as where your representatives can remain in the event that they need a break or wish to calm pressure. They can likewise take their workstations with them assuming they need a difference in view away from their work areas. Coordinated evenings out with the goal that your colleagues can become more acquainted with one another better, and structure kinships outside of work, they can empower cooperation back in the workplace. Your office ought to likewise mirror your image, brighten the spot, and ensure that it's appealing and fascinating while additionally remaining on brand. An examination from the financial expert announced that having a canine in the workplace can support usefulness and lessen pressure. Working with a canine close by additionally urged representatives to turn out to be better colleagues. concede your errors.

Genuine pioneers realize when to show lowliness and concede their slip-ups. By telling others that you are not great. You procure the admiration of your workers and carry yourself nearer to your group. Besides, it imparts unwaveringness in you.

Conceding your missteps likewise shows the strength of your person and urges your colleagues to not feel humiliated to concede any errors that they might make later on. Refine Your dynamic. Utilizing savvy instinct and settling on astute choices is one of the signs of being a decent supervisor. Rather than zeroing in on your preferred results, you should investigate the manner in which you concoct a particular game-plan. Also, compelling dynamic interaction includes the accompanying components. Quality requires breaking down the issue and contrasting the choices that are accessible with you. Execute capacity includes guaranteeing that your group is energetic about the alternative that you have decided to help the probability that your choice will be executed appropriately and make positive results. Time idealness implies guaranteeing that your choice is carried out at the ideal opportunity. be compassionate. Compassion alludes to the capacity to comprehend somebody's circumstance utilizing that equivalent individual's point of view. Being a compassionate administrator assists you with turning out to be more lenient toward different thoughts and feelings, assists creating with trusting and enduring connections and be more open to change. Here are a portion of the top explanations behind you to figure out how to be more sympathetic in the working environment. You can without much of a stretch perceive the sensations of your workers and control your activities likewise. You are more persuaded to follow a solid good compass based on correspondence, generosity, regard, and resistance.

You'll contemplate the necessities of your colleagues before you decide. You'll be more quiet and tolerating of analysis. You will not get cautious or factious in high pressure circumstances. You'll be more able to face challenges for the group since you esteem character over your self-image. Figure out how to isolate individual issues from association issues. In the event that you have assembled a confiding in relationship with your workers, they will come to you when they have issues. Be that as it may, you shouldn't treat these issues similarly. Understanding the contrast among individual and an authoritative issue will help you concoct a compelling reaction. You can address individual issues through your kin the executives' abilities without requiring extensive redesign. Then again, association issues are brought about by intrinsic issues inside the association. You'll have to assume responsibility for the circumstance. Converse with the senior chiefs about potential arrangements and keeping your staffs head above water until the issue is totally settled. check in consistently, in any event, when there's not all that much. Ensure that your workers can undoubtedly move toward you when they run over any issue or issue whatsoever. Work and check in with them intermittently. In any case, don't fly in or drift around such a lot of that it becomes upsetting or off-kilter. Along these lines, you can immediately extinguish fires before they turn gigantic. Customary one on one gatherings are likewise ideal with the goal that you can monitor their advancement, just as become acquainted with them better. Urge your representatives to be issue solvers. At a certain point or another, your group will experience apparently unthinkable circumstances. They'll stroll into your office and surrender things to you. This isn't the manner by which it ought to be finished.

Your job is to help productivity, not add on additional to your predicament. As their administrator, you ought to urge them to concoct potential arrangements before they come to you for help. following are some approaches to assist you with empowering critical thinking capacities inside your group. furnish them with adequate instruments, opportunity, and obligation to fix the issues that come their direction. trust them to take care of business. Try not to allow them to become reliant by not micromanaging. continually investigating their shoulder or continually rescuing them. Put forward objectives as opposed to giving them a rundown of guidelines. Allow them to sort out some way to finish the task as opposed to giving you an arrangement of steps that they can follow. support innovativeness. Since certain issues don't generally need a direct and consistent perspective. work with conceptualizing, collaboration is consistently something to be thankful for. In case there is an issue that your representative can't tackle all alone, take a stab at allowing him to cooperate with a gathering. improve at recognizing abilities. assigning errands requires having a strong handle of your group's ability pool, you ought to have the option to perceive your staff's abilities and gifts and tackle them so that would profit the whole association. Keep in mind, that not every person can deal with specific undertakings proficiently or effectively, so you ought to distinguish every part qualities and shortcomings. This will then, at that point assist you with making and dispense the assignments better and put together the work process all the more productively. Give individuals independence, it tends to be enticing to simply tell your representatives precisely what you need them to do. This can work in circumstances where the representatives unfit to meet your normal nature of work. Be that as it may, most workers favor being free and like to be tested. Permit your representatives to assume liability and responsibility for their work. Here are some approaches to energize self-sufficiency with your colleagues.

challenge them yet ensure that they don't get overpowered, set up limits. While self-governance is for the most part something worth being thankful for, an excessive amount of decision can likewise be hazardous. Leave your workers alone self-ruling, yet additionally consider them responsible for the outcomes. set out open doors for your group to find out about getting sorted out, adjusting needs, and objective setting. Self-governance doesn't mean totally forsaking them. Ensure that you're generally there to offer guidance and backing. Try not to hide issues away from plain view. At whatever point you experience issues inside the group or the association. Try not to sneak around them. All things being equal, deal with them directly and never wonder whether or not to move forward. Think of potential arrangements before it antagonistically influences your group. Remember that an antipathy for awkward circumstances shouldn't hold you back from battling for your group and paying special mind to any issue that may undermine their prosperity and nature of work. Your workers need you to go to bat for them with the goal that they can tackle their responsibilities to the guidelines you've set. be responsive to negative input. Try not to respond protectively in the event that you get negative input. Truth be told, consistently expect that the individual who gave this has an honest goal.

It's essentially exactly the same thing as giving input and analysis to any colleague isn't performing admirably. You need them to learn and work on similarly that they need you to help them change things. Assuming nobody in your group needs to approach with a legitimate analysis, change your methodology.

Rather than requesting criticism. Ask them for guidance. Here and there individuals see the word criticism with negative focal points. It can appear to be too formal or constrained asking your group for counsel shows your faith in their insight and abilities to deal with poisonous workers.

Indeed, even all those administrators can get burdened with that one representative that makes work life hopeless for individuals around them. On the off chance that you can't let him, go promptly, here are some extraordinary approaches to react to their conduct and decrease the harm they cause. distinguish the reason for their discontent. Is it accurate to say that they are discontent with their job? Or then again would they say they are encountering misfortunes in their own life? meet with them to discover what their explanation is and offer to help. Ensure that you let them know straightforwardly the impact they have in the remainder of their group. harmful individuals can be careless in regard to their environmental elements since they are too centered around themselves and their issues. Timetable one on one gatherings with the remainder of the group to get the opposite side of the story. foster a game plan to address the circumstance. On the off chance that the poisonous worker is as yet impervious to change, acknowledge the way that you will not have the option to fix things and investigate different alternatives. archive the conduct, the means you have taken, any authority alerts you have given, and the grievances from the remainder of the group. Continuously be on schedule. Regardless of whether you were simply meeting casually with your colleagues adhere to the settled upon plan. This shows that you regard their time as profoundly as you esteem yours. It will likewise assist with advancing trust and regard and one another. In case you are routinely late to your group gatherings, maybe it's an ideal opportunity to take a glance at your time usage abilities. Regardless of whether you need to stop a past gathering arrive as expected. On the off chance that you realize that you will be late, ensure that you illuminate them something like an hour in advance. Focus on wellbeing and prosperity solid workers are contributing representatives. Studies show that probably the greatest wellspring of shortcoming and usefulness misfortune are debilitated workers. Ensure that you urge your representatives to take some personal time every so often to de pressure and restore. Show others how it's done through taking your days off, focusing on personal time, and putting your wellbeing first. Recollect that you ought to never give your representatives that functioning 24 seven is the lone way they can make progress in the association.

oversee assumptions. At times customers and bosses will push for results and cutoff times that are simply not achievable. In cases like this, let your supervisors know what your group is reasonably equipped for achieving. Given their ideal result and existing responsibility. Give them a more feasible picture. Telling your bosses when something isn't sensible, would assist them with changing their assumptions or, in any event, give you instruments and assets that you can use to work quicker and all the more productively. Furthermore, presently it's conversation time. The main piece of this preparation whoever's the big boss in the gathering should assign a facilitator whose obligation it is that every one of the inquiries you see on your screen is covered and that everybody time allowing, can give their opinion, ensure all commitments are esteemed. All ideas considered, and all sentiments regarded.

Don't miss out!

Visit the website below and you can sign up to receive emails whenever B. Vincent publishes a new book. There's no charge and no obligation.

https://books2read.com/r/B-A-QWUO-THCRB

BOOKS 2 READ

Connecting independent readers to independent writers.

Also by B. Vincent

Affiliate Marketing
Affiliate Marketing
Affiliate Marketing

Standalone
Business Employee Discipline
Affiliate Recruiting
Business Layoffs & Firings
Business and Entrepreneur Guide
Business Remote Workforce
Career Transition
Project Management
Precision Targeting
Professional Development
Strategic Planning
Content Marketing
Imminent List Building
Getting Past GateKeepers
Banner Ads

Bookkeeping
Bridge Pages
Business Acquisition
Business Bogging
Marketing Automation
Better Meetings
Conversion Optimization
Creative Solutions
Employee Recruitment
Startup Capital
Employee Mentoring
Followership
Servant Leadership
Human Resources
Team Building
Freelancing
Funnel Building
Geo Targeting
Goal Setting
Immanent List Building
Lead Generation
Leadership Course
Leadership Transition
LinkedIn Ads
LinkedIn Marketing
New Management

About the Publisher

Accepting manuscripts in the most categories. We love to help people get their words available to the world.

Revival Waves of Glory focus is to provide more options to be published. We do traditional paperbacks, hardcovers, audio books and ebooks all over the world. A traditional royalty-based publisher that offers self-publishing options, Revival Waves provides a very author friendly and transparent publishing process, with President Bill Vincent involved in the full process of your book. Send us your manuscript and we will contact you as soon as possible.

Contact: Bill Vincent at rwgpublishing@yahoo.com www.rwgpublishing.com

www.ingramcontent.com/pod-product-compliance
Lightning Source LLC
Chambersburg PA
CBHW030536210326
41597CB00014B/1171